Backyard Scientist®

Exploring Earthworms with Me

by Jane Hoffman

Illustrated by Lanny Ostroff

The Backyard Scientist Series includes:

The Original Backyard Scientist. This widely read and popular book was the author's first writing effort and features exciting hands-on science experiments to interest children ages 4 through 12 in science. A great beginning science book.

Backyard Scientist, Series One. The author's second book of hands-on science experiments provides children ages 4 through 12 with more fascinating and fun ways to explore the world of science.

Backyard Scientist, Series Two is the writer's third book. It is geared for children ages 9 through 14 years and features a special collection of exciting, fascinating and challenging hands-on experiments.

Backyard Scientist, Series Three. This is the author's fourth book and it teaches young scientists ages 4 through 12 about the living world with hands-on experiments in biology, physiology, entomology and more.

Backyard Scientist, Series Four is the author's fifth book in the award-winning series. Containing exciting and stimulating hands-on experiments for scientists of all ages, it is excellent for classroom, group, family and individual scientific investigations.

Backyard Scientist, Exploring Earthworms with Me
April 1994

Library of Congress catalog number: 94-094-146

Published by Backyard Scientist/Jane Hoffman
P. O. Box 16966, Irvine, CA 92713

0-9618663-5-7

Backyard Scientist, Exploring Earthworms with Me
is dedicated to Millie Weinstein (my 98-year-old grandmother).

The Reviews Are in

What Educators, Parents, and the Media

*"For the easiest and most enjoyable approach to science experiments, I recommend **The Backyard Scientist** by Jane Hoffman."*
Mary Pride
The Teaching Home

"Her goal [is] to see the public school system adopt an ongoing, daily, hands-on science curriculum. No one can say that Jane Hoffman isn't doing her part to try to achieve this aim."
Nita Kurmins Gilson
The Christian Science Monitor

*"Hoffman's own curiosity and energy are a large part of the appeal of **The Backyard Scientist.** I believe that science makes a difference in the way a child learns."*
The Chicago Tribune

*"Anyone who can read, or get an assistant to read, can have fun building the experiments described in **The Backyard Scientist** series and then have even more fun using [Hoffman's] experiments to explore science."*
Paul Doherty, Ph.D
Physicist/Teacher

"What makes these experiments special is their hands-on nature. A firm believer that science makes a difference in how a child learns, Hoffman encourages kids to think for themselves, to ask questions and to observe the world around them."
Science Books and Films

"All of the experiments have been pre-tested extensively with groups of children."
Curriculum Product News Magazine

"I believe that you have many of the answers to our problems with science education in the early grades."
Mary Kohleman
National Science Foundation
Washington, DC

"There are a lot of good reasons why you should order the books, but if you need another one, just remember you're doing it for a worthy cause…your students."
Teaching K-8 Magazine

"Popcorn, ice cubes and string are among the materials used in her experiments…most of which the children conduct themselves. But the main ingredient is the enthusiasm that Jane generates in the fledgling scientist."
Woman's Day Magazine

*"…[**Backyard Scientist** series] is the best 'hands-on' experience a young reader can help him- or herself to. Original and highly recommended for schools and home-teaching."*
Children's Bookwatch

"As a teacher, I truly appreciated your book. It was well organized and easy to follow. The experience with a variety of scientific concepts has sparked further interest in several areas with many of the students. They have asked for more!"
Amy Korenack
Resource Teacher

"She makes science come alive."
Orange Coast Daily Pilot

*"**Backyard Scientist** teaches the art of thinking."*
Anaheim Bulletin

"My mom is a teacher and thinks these books are the greatest!"
Ryan, age 5

*"I loved the **Backyard Scientist** series. I like things I hadn't thought of doing my myself."*
Chris, age 7

on Backyard Scientist

Are Saying about the Backyard Scientist

"I loved the **Backyard Scientist** books. They are so great."

Thomas, age 8½

"I tried your experiments with my students and they went wild with excitement."

First Grade Teacher
Illinois

"I really appreciate the clear instructions, simple-to-get household supplies, and the complete and easy-to-understand explanations. Thanks for these wonderful books."

Mrs. Getz
Home Schooling Mom

"Any serious young scientist and his or her equally serious parents will find Hoffman's carefully designed science book useful. The experiments are carefully labeled as to outcomes, so that you know before you start, for example, that the "Car Experiment" is about friction, gravity, oxidation, and lubrication. The result is the kind of visually interesting science experiment that engrossed you during a well-run science lab in grade or junior high school. One suspects that more than one overworked and underpaid middle school teacher is going to be using this book as an unofficial science lab book and text throughout the year. The directions are exceedingly thorough, and each experiment has a list of questions for young scientist to answer through their own observations."

Pat Wagner
The Bloomsbury Review

"Hoffman prefaces her collection with good advice such as: 'Always work with an adult and never taste anything you are experimenting with (unless specifically instructed to do so).' Experiments include practice in growing mold and splitting the atom. Just kidding about the last, though Hoffman does include an experiment using a drop of oil that simulates the effect of atomic fission."

Michael Dirda
The Washington Post

"Jane Hoffman is doing her part to make chemistry and physics come alive for Americans ages 4 through 12."

Newsmaker Interviews

"Can popcorn float on bubbles? Does sound travel through liquids? These questions may sound silly to adults, but kids love to find out the answers, says educator Jane Hoffman in the book **Backyard Scientist.**"

Michael Dale Wireless Flash News
Copley Radio Network

"I just want to let you know how much we enjoy your book, **Backyard Scientist**. As a mother of eight I really appreciate the clear instructions that allow a child to work independently, from collecting materials through the questions that foster creative thinking and deductive reasoning. I'm waiting to see your next book."

Jan Vreeland
Waukesha, WI

"All the experiments are ones that are simple enough for a child to carry out himself (with a helpful parent nearby), and Jane is careful to use only materials commonly found around most homes. Often follow-up ideas are given for further exploration and an explanation of the hows and whys."

Susan Richman
Pennsylvania Homeschoolers

"The **Backyard Scientist** is exceptional in its flexibility to be used with children ages 4 through 12. This quality is especially helpful for those teaching multi-grade levels. I would recommend this book to any family that wants science to be active, educational and fun."

Roxanne Smith
Grand Rapids, MI

Acknowledgements

Thanks to my husband Arnold and son Jason for their encouragement and research help. They had to look up the definition of dinner in the dictionary several times while I was writing this book.

A special thanks to Sid and Grace Goldsmith, my parents, for their important contributions in getting this book ready for publication.

You would not be reading this page without the encouragement and positive feedback from the teachers, parents, and scientists-to-be. Thank you for your continuing enthusiastic support.

Preface

Welcome to *Exploring Earthworms With Me*. Through the exciting hands-on experiments in this book we will investigate this interesting creature from scientific and ecological perspectives. Remember, you will be working with living creatures, so be sure to handle them with care and respect. Always, always return the earthworms to their natural habitat after you have completed an experiment. Gather new earthworms for each experiment.

As soon as you begin experimenting, you become a Backyard Scientist working in the real world of scientific investigation. Your laboratory is wherever you are experimenting, be it in your backyard, kitchen or basement.

As a Backyard Scientist working in your laboratory, there are some very important guidelines you must follow. These are found on the Rules page of this book. Read them carefully before you begin experimenting.

Good—now you are ready to start experimenting. Have fun! When you complete all of the experiments be sure to read how you can get your Backyard Scientist Certificate and how to join the Backyard Scientist Club. It's free. Details are on page 45.

Parents and teachers, I hope you will continue to encourage your students to explore the world around them using this and the other *Backyard Scientist* books of hands-on experimenting. It is through hands-on investigations that youngsters will view science in an enthusiastic and positive way. It is also the best way to learn about this interesting subject.

Happy Experimenting,

Jane Hoffman

Your Friend,
Jane Hoffman
The Backyard Scientist

Backyard Scientist Rules for Experimenting

- Young children must always have an adult with them when they are experimenting.
- Older children must always have an adult nearby when experimenting.
- Always wash your hands after each experiment.
- Never eat anything you are experimenting with except when instructed to do so by an adult.
- Always read all the instructions before beginning the experiment, and then follow each step as instructed.
- Always keep your earthworms in the dark or in a dimly lighted room. Earthworms like temperatures of around 50 degrees Fahrenheit.

YOU WILL BE WORKING WITH LIVING THINGS. ALWAYS TREAT THEM GENTLY AND WITH RESPECT. KEEP THE EARTHWORMS ONLY AS LONG AS YOU WANT TO CARE FOR THEM. ALWAYS RETURN THE EARTHWORMS TO THEIR NATURAL HABITAT.

Now, have fun while learning about these interesting creatures!

Be Kind to the Environment: Recycling Ideas for Your Experiments

Be environmentally sound by collecting styrofoam food containers, cottage cheese containers, see-through salad containers and so on to use in your experiments.

For example, substitute styrofoam food containers for baking sheets and see-through food containers for zip-close bags. Be sure your recycled containers have been washed with water. DO NOT USE SOAP.

Space on each experiment page does not allow me to list all the recycling possibilities, but be creative and recycle whenever possible.

We all care about our environment and should try and be environmentally sound whenver we can. If you come up with any other creative substitutes to use in the experiments, please write to me so I can share them with others.

CAUTION

The subject matter of this work is based on the scientific. The author is specific in directions, explanations and warnings. If what is written is disregarded, failure or complications may occur—just as is the case in the laboratory. In the instances where flammable or toxic chemicals are involved, explicit explanations and warnings are provided.

Contents

Supplies List

Here is a list of all the supplies you will need to do the experiments in this book. You won't need all the supplies at one time. My suggestion is to go through your home and check off what supplies you have on hand. Then slowly gather the other supplies. Be sure to read the supplies section of all the experiments. Several of the supplies listed below can be used for more than one experiment. Some supplies are used in several experiments.

Adults to help you

Sheet of plastic

Small shovel

Friends

Earthworms (Get new worms for each experiment since you will be releasing the earthworms to their natural habitat after each experiment.)

Damp soil

Watering can

Paper towels

Baking pan with sides

See-through measuring cups

Magnifying lens (optional)

Ruler

Small nail

Notebook paper (a sheet for each experiment)

Pencil

Poster board

Large piece of paper, tissue paper, and wax paper

Newspapers

Clear tape

Paper towels

Radio or tape player

Any kind of musical or noise-making instruments (harmonica, whistle, drum, pots or pans, and a piano if you have one)

Three potted plants

String

Tape measure

Ice cream sticks

Flashlight

Different colors of cellophane or plastic wrap

Clean, empty coffee can

Clean, empty cottage cheese container

Clean, empty yogurt container

Clean, empty milk carton

Clean, empty gallon plastic jar or peanut butter jar

Plastic bowl

Lawn or access to a park with grass

Piece of cardboard (8½ by 11 inches or legal size)

Water

Black paper (8½ by 11 inches)

Large deep container with a large opening

Fresh leaves from a variety of shrubs and trees

Decomposed leaves

Celery leaves, carrot tops, lettuce, cabbage, turnip greens, baby food, cornmeal or bread crumbs, fruit peelings, brown sugar and coffee grounds (You only need three or four of these items.)

Several zip-close plastic bags

Labels

White paper plate (dinner size)

Different kinds of sand such as construction sand, river sand (DO NOT USE BEACH SAND—IT IS TOO SALTY.)

Sheet of clear acetate 24 x 20 inches

Small piece of plastic screen material

Rubber bands

Fine gravel

Aluminum foil

3 or 4 cups of good garden soil

3 or 4 cups of peat moss

Let's Start Experimenting!

(Don't forget to read the Rules page (viii) before proceeding.)

Hunting for Earthworms

Gather the following supplies:

a sheet of wax paper and a small shovel, a plastic container or plastic bag, damp soil, damp moss, some friends, and your observation skills.

Start experimenting.

1. Invite your friends to go on an earthworm hunt. Look for your worms in gardens, fields and compost piles. Where else can you find worms?
2. During the day, place the sheet of wax paper on the ground in an area where the soil is moist and cool. You can also look for other areas of the yard to place the wax paper.
3. With the small shovel, carefully dig up some soil and place it on the sheet of wax paper. **Remember, always get permission before you dig up a yard.**
4. To find earthworms, search through the soil on the wax paper by gently moving the soil around with the shovel.
5. With an adult, at night, repeat steps 3 and 4 of this experiment.

Can you answer the following questions from your observations?

1. Did you find any earthworms on your sheet of wax paper during your daytime search?
2. Did you find any earthworms on your sheet of wax paper during your nighttime search?
3. What different kinds of places did you look for earthworms? Did you find any there?
4. Can you think of at least three places in which earthworms are likely to live?
5. Which is better for finding earthworms, dry soil or moist soil?
6. Do you think you would find more or fewer earthworms after it rained?

Backyard Scientist Solution:

Earthworms live in small-diameter tubes inside the earth. The earth must be moist or the worm, with its porous skin, will lose all of its moisture to the dry soil. This is why hunting for earthworms in moist places is best. Earthworms have certain characteristics that enable them to live in these defined niches. These include environmental factors such as light, temperature, moisture and pressure. In situations where temperature change is somewhat gradual or seasonal, the worm can burrow to a more hospitable level. If the temperature drops too low, the worm's metabolism also drops greatly. The worm could get so cold that it could not move or eat.

When too much water enters a worm tunnel, the tunnel can become blocked with debris or plug up completely. The worm loses some of the friction necessary to crawl or wiggle forward, and its gas exchange (oxygen in, carbon dioxide out) is restricted. The worm responds to large concentrations of water in the tunnel by trying to avoid them and escape to a more habitable tunnel, or to a protected location above ground. After a heavy rain, worms can be picked up off sidewalks where they go to avoid drowning in the waterlogged soil.

The earthworm's skin senses light, and worms can tell when it is day or night. They are nocturnal animals and rarely come out of the ground except at night, so they prefer a dark environment to a light one. The earthworm hunts for food at night. That is why it is called "nightcrawler." Its food is fallen leaves and animal debris. It usually extends its body from a small burrow which it creates by literally eating its way through the soil. The hind part of the worm's body remains near the surface end of the burrow while the rest of the animal forages for food.

After finding your earthworms, use a plastic container or bag with some damp soil for transporting and maintaining the worms.

If you live in a place where you do not have access to a yard or other places that earthworms frequent, you will have to find other resources for finding the worms to experiment with. You could buy them at a bait shop or from places that grow earthworms for sale. One such place is a company called Insect Lore. You can get more information by calling 1-800-LIVE BUG or writing them at P.O. Box 1535, Shafter, CA 93263. You can also ask fishermen about good places to get worms. They may even give you some for experimenting.

You can keep a lot of worms on hand for experimenting. The best way to keep them is in a large, clean, empty cottage cheese container or a large, clean, empty yogurt container. Punch small holes in the top, get some damp moss, and keep your earthworms in these containers in the refrigerator. Earthworms will keep up to one month like this in the refrigerator. **Be sure to label the containers.**

Observing the Earthworm

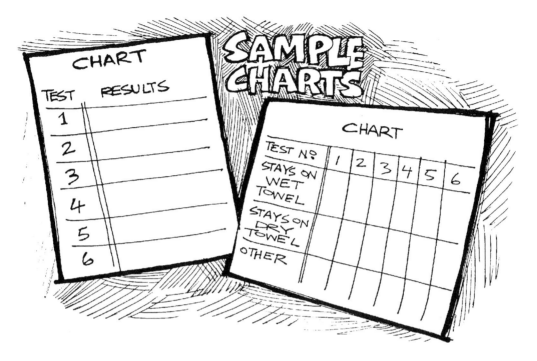

Gather the following supplies:

several earthworms, damp soil, a baking pan with sides, a magnifying lens (optional), and some friends to help you.

Start experimenting.

SPECIAL NOTE: Never put your earthworms in direct sunlight as it might kill them.

1. Place the damp soil on the baking pan.
2. Place the earthworms on top of the soil.
3. Observe the earthworms and their actions very carefully.
4. Observe all parts of the earthworms very carefully. Use the magnifying lens for this if you have one.
5. Pick up an earthworm and examine it very carefully.
6. Try turning the earthworm over and gently run your finger over the bottom side of the worm.
7. Take your time and watch very carefully while the worm moves along.

Can you answer the following questions from your observations?

1. Do earthworms have a head?
2. Do earthworms have eyes?
3. Do earthworms have a nose and ears?
4. Do earthworms have a mouth?
5. Do earthworms have arms or legs?
6. Do earthworms have a tail?
7. Do all earthworms look alike?
8. Do earthworms seem to have bones?
9. What part of the earthworm's body enables it to move along?
10. Do you think earthworms are very strong?
11. Do you think earthworms have muscles?
12. Do you think earthworms have backbones?
13. Do you know the name for animals without a backbone?
14. Do you know what the main sensing organ of the earthworm is called?

Backyard Scientist solution:

Based on your observations, did you discover that your earthworms have no eyes, ears, arms, tail, bones or legs? Earthworms have a mouth and head. The earthworm has two sets of muscles. One set is the circular muscle which is located around each segment. The other is a set of long muscles that run the length of the body. When the circular muscles tighten, the earthworm becomes longer and thinner. When the lengthwise muscles tighten, the earthworm becomes shorter and fatter.

An earthworm is a lower invertebrate (an animal without a backbone). The earthworm's body is made up of many segments which appear as rings. Older worms have more segments than younger worms. The adult worm has a thick, whitish band around its body.

The head of an earthworm is thicker than the tail end. Earthworms have a very sensitive nose that is used for smelling decaying organic material which is the worms food source. The main sensing organ of worms is their skin. The worm's skin is very sensitive and responds to moisture, temperature, touch and light. The worm uses its skin to see, hear, detect moisture and feel.

On the underside of the earthworm you will find bristles. These bristles are called *setae*. There are four pairs on all but the first and last segments. The bristles are made of *chitin*, which is the same material the hard outer covering of insects is composed of. These bristles help the worm dig into the soil when it moves and help the earthworms cling to the sides of the burrow when predators try to pull them out. The earthworm's predators are robins and other birds, frogs, centipedes, moles and man. A protective adaptation is the worm's brownish color. This makes the worm harder to see against the soil. Earthworms have different shadings caused by variations in the pigments of their skin.

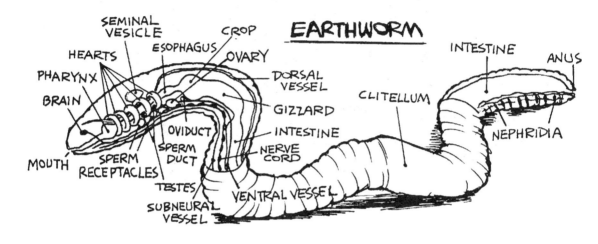

EARTHWORM

SEMINAL VESICLE
CROP
ESOPHAGUS
OVARY
HEARTS
PHARYNX
BRAIN
DORSAL VESSEL
GIZZARD
INTESTINE
CLITELLUM
INTESTINE
ANUS
OVIDUCT
SPERM DUCT
NERVE CORD
NEPHRIDIA
MOUTH
SPERM RECEPTACLES
TESTES
VENTRAL VESSEL
SUBNEURAL VESSEL

Measuring an Earthworm

Gather the following supplies:

several earthworms, some damp soil, a baking pan with sides, a ruler, paper, and pencil.

Start experimenting.

1. Place the damp soil on the baking pan.
2. Now place an earthworm on the soil.
3. With the ruler, measure the earthworm at its most stretched-out position as it moves along the baking pan.
4. Also, measure the earthworm when it is in its shortest position.
5. Repeat steps 2, 3, and 4 until all your earthworms have been measured.
6. Record your observations.

Can you answer the following questions from your observations?

1. Do you think all earthworms are the same length?
2. Was it hard to accurately measure the length of the earthworms?
3. Does the length of the earthworm change as it moves along?

Backyard Scientist solution:

Earthworms come in many different sizes, just like people, plants and other animals. They are very difficult to measure with any accuracy as they move along. The earthworm's body is short and fat. In order to move, a worm stretches itself out and becomes long and thin, and then it pulls itself together and looks shorter and fatter.

The same worm can measure 2 inches long when it is all pulled together, and then when it stretches, it could measure 6 inches. Also, the length of the earthworm will depend on how many segments the worm has. The older the worm, the more segments it has.

Earthworms have two sets of muscles. The circular muscles are around each segment. The long muscles run the length of the body. When the circular muscles tighten, the earthworm becomes longer and thinner. When the long muscles tighten, the earthworm becomes shorter and fatter.

For further research you might want to go to the library and find the answers to the following questions. What is the scientific name of the longest worm, and in what part of the country would you find this worm?

Do Earthworms Make Noise?

Gather the following supplies:

poster board or a large piece of paper, tissue paper, wax paper, aluminum foil, newspapers and several earthworms. You will need a very quiet place to conduct this experiment. Keeping the results of this experiment will be exciting.

Start Experimenting.

1. Place one of your earthworms on each of the surfaces listed in the supply list.
2. Carefully listen to the earthworm as it moves over the different surfaces you place it on.
3. Make mental or written notes about your observations.
4. Repeat the same experiments with the other earthworms.
5. If you have a portable recorder and microphone, you might try recording any noise the earthworm makes, and then play the tape back at a high volume setting.

Can you answer the following questions from your observations?

1. Did you hear any noises made by the earthworms?
2. Were the earthworms still or moving when you heard the noises?
3. Were the noises frequent?
4. Were the noises loud?
5. What kind of noises did you hear? Describe them.
6. Do you know how the noises were made by the earthworms?
7. Were the noises the same on all the surfaces, or were there different noises depending on which surface you placed your earthworm on?

Backyard Scientist solution:

You discovered the earthworm made a scratching sound as it moved over the poster board, and it definitely made different noises as it moved across the different surfaces. It did not make any noise when it was not moving. The noise you heard was made by the bristles (hard little hairs) on the earthworm's body. These bristles are on almost every segment of the earthworm's body. The bristles help the earthworm move by giving it traction on slippery surfaces. If a surface is too rough, the earthworm may have trouble moving because it will not have any traction.

Remember, never use the same earthworm too long for any one experiment. Keep using different earthworms. Always make sure your earthworms stay moist and their skins do not dry out.

Do You Think Earthworms Can Hear?

Gather the following supplies:

a baking pan with sides or a styrofoam container, moist paper towels, a radio or tape player, any kind of musical instrument(s) you have (harmonica, whistle or a drum will do and a piano or access to one will help), a couple of old pots or pans and something to strike them with, two or three earthworms, and a potted plant with damp soil.

Start Experimenting.

1. Place the damp paper towels in the baking pan or a styrofoam container. Add the earthworms. Be sure the towels are damp so the earthworms' skin does not dry out, so they can breathe (respire). We don't want to injure the earthworms.
2. Begin playing the radio or tape player at ever increasing volume. Observe the earthworms carefully for any kind of reaction to the sound.
3. Now play the musical instruments one at a time. Bang on the pots too. Observe for any reaction to the sound.
4. If you are doing this experiment indoors, jump up and down close to the earthworms.
5. Remove the earthworms from the container and place them in the potted plant.
6. Place the potted plant with the earthworms on the piano, and play the piano. Observe the earthworms.

Can you answer the following questions from your observations?

1. Did the earthworms show any reaction to the sounds you generated?
2. Which sounds did the earthworms react to?
3. Did the volume of the sound impact the reaction of the earthworms?
4. How did the earthworms react to the sounds?
5. As we know, earthworms do not have ears. How do they sense that moles (which like to eat earthworms) are nearby?
6. Do you think earthworms hear sounds through the air like you and other humans and animals do?

Backyard Scientist Solution:

Earthworms cannot hear sound in the same way humans and many other animals hear sound. However, earthworms are very sensitive to vibrations that are transmitted through the soil. Sound waves can be felt as vibrations. Bang on the pot and then touch the pot with your finger. Can you feel the pot vibrating?

Some people who raise earthworms for fishing bait say they can make earthworms come to the surface of the beds they are raised in by banging on a pot held near the surface. The earthworms may be thinking the vibration they feel is a nearby mole wanting to make a meal of them, so they head to the surface for safety.

You should have noticed that the earthworms reacted more to some noises than to others. In most cases, you will find the greatest response is to the sound of the piano. This is because the pot and soil are strong conductors of the vibrations produced by the piano. The earthworms were highly stimulated by these strong vibrations.

How Many Earthworms, Do You Think, Are in a Patch of Grass?

Gather the following supplies:

string, tape measure, ice cream sticks, flashlight covered with red cellophane, a watering can (you can make your own by having an adult punch a few holes in the bottom of an empty coffee can), a plastic bowl, some water, a pencil and paper, and a patch of lawn you can use.

Start experimenting.

1. Measure an area 3 feet on each side (1 square yard). Pound the ice cream sticks into the corners of the area. Mark the entire area by wrapping the string around the corner markers.
2. At sunset, water the area. This will bring the earthworms to the surface when it gets dark.
3. Predict how many earthworms you think are in your experimenting area. Record your prediction.
4. After it is dark, use the red flashlight to find the earthworms in your marked area. Pick them up gently and place them into the collecting bowl. Pick up all you can find, then count them and release them. Record the number you collected.
5. Repeat the experiment on another patch of lawn at another time and record your observations.

Can you answer the following questions from your observations?

1. How many earthworms did you collect?
2. Was the number collected close to the number predicted?
3. Did different areas of the lawn have about the same number of earthworms?
4. What was the average number of earthworms in the areas you measured? (Total number of earthworms found divided by number of areas measured).
5. How might you mathematically estimate how many earthworms are in the total lawn?

Backyard Scientist solution:

You probably found lots of earthworms if it was not too cold. To find the number of earthworms that might be in your lawn, multiply the average number of earthworms you found by the number of square yards in your lawn. Measure the width times the length of your lawn, in feet, and divide by nine to get square yards (1 square yard equals 9 square feet). After a heavy rain, you may see hundreds of earthworms on a lawn, driveway or sidewalk.

Do Earthworms Like to Be Kept in Jars?

Gather the following supplies:

a large jar you can see through (a clean gallon plastic jar or plastic peanut butter jar works well for this experiment), damp garden soil or peat moss, (avoid soils that are hard or compact), a fine sand and gravel (don't use sand from an ocean beach because it is very salty), three to six earthworms, several partially decomposed leaves or fresh leaves cut in small pieces, coffee grounds and brown sugar, a piece of black paper to fit around the jar, a piece of plastic screen to cover the top of the jar, a rubber band, and a pencil and paper for notes.

NOTE: This experiment will take seven days.

Start experimenting.

1. Place a ½-inch layer of fine gravel in the bottom of the jar for drainage.
2. Add a ½-inch layer of garden soil on top of the gravel. Keep the soil moist, but not soaked.
3. Add a ½-inch layer of fine sand on top of the soil
4. Repeat steps 2 and 3 until the jar is nearly full. Add the coffee grounds and brown sugar last.
5. Place the earthworms in the jar and add the leaves.
6. Cover the jar with the plastic screen. Use a rubber band to seal the screen.
7. Place the black paper around the outside of the jar so the earthworms will be in a dark environment, the same as if they were in their own habitat.
8. During the time you will be waiting, what do you think the earthworms will be doing? Make some predictions and write them down.
9. Keep the worms in the dark for about 7 days. Then remove the black paper from the outside of the jar. Carefully observe what took place during this period.

Can you answer the following questions from your observations?

1. What happened to the leaves you placed in the jar?
2. What happened to the alternating layers of soil and sand you made before adding the earthworms to the jar?
3. Do you think the earthworms like being in the jar?
4. In what other places do you think the earthworms would prefer to be?

Backyard Scientist solution:

You will have noticed the earthworms were very busy and active during the seven-day waiting period. During that time the worms literally ate through the soil to make tubes and tunnels, thus mixing up the different layers of soil. Moist soil makes it easier for them to make tunnels, which means they consume more food per minute. The decomposed leaves (organic material) that you placed on top of the soil and sand were eaten by the worms in the first days to give them the energy they needed to begin their burrows.

As long as your earthworms are comfortable and have food, they will be very happy to stay in the jar. If you keep the earthworms in the jar longer than a week, be sure to keep their home clean. Check the soil for young worms. Do not let the jar become over-populated with worms. Put your extra worms in other containers or return them to their natural habitat. Discard any food that has a bad smell or is moldy. Do not overfeed your worms. Two tablespoons of food or leaves every other week is enough food. Always keep your worms in the darkest and coolest place in your home. Earthworms like temperatures that are around 50 degrees Fahrenheit. You can also cover the jar with damp rags to keep it cool. However, like any caged animal, they would prefer to be in their natural habitat.

Do Earthworms Like Dry or Damp Places?

Gather the following supplies:

a baking pan with sides, two paper towels, cardboard large enough to cover the pan you use, water, paper and pencil, and ten to twelve earthworms.

Start experimenting.

1. Make a chart, or have someone help you make a chart, to record your results.
2. Place a dry paper towel on one end of your flat pan.
3. Wet another paper towel and wring it out so it is still damp. Place the damp paper towel next to the dry paper towel.
4. Put a worm on one of the towels near the overlapping edges. Watch for a while observing the worm to see where it goes.
5. Now cover the pan with the piece of cardboard. Just place it loosely over the pan. Wait about ½ hour, uncover the pan, and observe what the earthworm is doing.

6. Take another worm and do the experiment again.
7. You can alter this experiment by putting three or four worms on the wet side and three or four worms on the dry side, and then observing what happens.
8. Repeat this experiment several times.
9. Remember, always use different worms for each experiment because their protective body coating is removed with heavy handling. They need this coating to respire (breathe).

Can you answer the following questions from your observations?

1. Which side were the earthworms on before you covered the pan?
2. When you removed the cover of the pan, were the earthworms gathered on the dry paper towel or on the damp paper towel?
3. Based on this observation, do you think you will find earthworms in dry soil or in damp soil?
4. Why do earthworms prefer to be in damp soil?
5. If you tried using three or four worms on each side, where did most of the worms end up?

Backyard Scientist solution:

You will have discovered the earthworms have moved to the side of the pan with the damp paper towel. Earthworms thrive best when they are in damp soil. If their bodies get too dry, the earthworms will dehydrate and finally die. Because birds and other small animals use earthworms for food, the earthworms usually remain in their burrows during daylight hours. They only come out at night when they cannot be easily seen by their predators. This makes them *nocturnal* animals.

You can also try doing this same experiment using dry soil and wet soil. Remember, always use more than one worm and try each experiment several times to be sure of avoiding abnormal behavior.

Dry soil, you will see, dries out the moist body covering of the worm. When this happens, return the worm to moist soil right away.

Do Earthworms Like Light?

CARD-BOARD →

Gather the following supplies:

one baking pan with sides, paper towels and water to dampen them, cardboard large enough to cover half the pan, paper and pencil, and about six earthworms.

Start experimenting.

1. With the pencil and paper, make a chart for recording your results indicating whether your worms stay in the light area or the dark area. You can have an adult help you make the chart.

2. Cover the bottom of the pan with damp paper towels.

3. Place the pan near a window that gets a lot of sunlight. **Remember, never put a worm in direct sunlight.**

4. Cover half of the pan with the cardboard.
5. Take one of your worms and place it in the middle of the pan. Watch it for a little while, and when your worm has decided on a place to stay, record it on your chart.
6. Now take out another worm and repeat the experiment.
7. If you wish you may use three or four worms at a time.

Can you answer the following questions from your observations?

1. Where did the earthworms go first? Did they stay there?
2. On which side of the pan did they end up—the side that had the cardboard cover or the side where the light could reach them?
3. Do earthworms have eyes?
4. If not, how do you suppose they can tell light from dark?

Backyard Scientist solution:

Did you discover that most of the time your earthworms moved to the side of the pan covered with cardboard? They do not like to be in the light. It is possible that the earthworms stayed in the middle of the pan where you placed them, neither moving to the dark area or more fully into the lighted area. Sometimes they may even try to get out of the pan and escape. Be sure to note this unusual behavior on your observation sheet. Scientists always repeat their experiments to insure that consistent results are achieved. Use some other earthworms and see if you get the same results.

You should repeat experiments and use several different worms to make sure that what you saw the first time wasn't an accident. Suppose you picked out earthworms that were very frightened; then they would not act in their usual way.

Generally, earthworms remain in their burrows and only come out of them at night. Earthworms do not have eyes. They are, however, sensitive to light and vibrations.

Are Earthworms Sensitive to Different Colors of Light?

RESPONSE	TAIL	MIDDLE	HEAD
NO MOVEMENT			
SLIGHT MOVEMENT			
GREAT MOVEMENT			

Gather the following supplies:

a flashlight with good batteries, a small nail, an 8½ x 11-inch piece of black paper, several vivid colors (red, green, blue, yellow, etc.) of clear plastic wrap or cellophane, an adult to help you, and pencil and paper for recording your observations.

Start experimenting.

1. Cut the black paper to the size of the flashlight lens so the lens is completely covered. Use the small nail to put a small hole as close as possible to the center of this lens cover. Tape the paper to the flashlight. This will allow a tiny beam of light to be emitted from the flashlight.
2. Ask an adult to accompany you on an earthworm hunt. The best time and place to do this experiment is on a lawn or field on a warm, damp night.
3. Carefully tiptoe on the lawn or field until you spot an earthworm. Watch the earthworm from a distance before going closer.

4. When you get close to the earthworm, shine the flashlight and aim the beam of light on the tail end of the earthworm. Observe what is taking place.
5. Slowly move the beam along the earthworm's body to its head. Observe how different parts of the earthworm react to the light.
6. Cover the black flashlight lens with one of the plastic wrap or cellophane colors.
7. Find some more earthworms to further experiment with the different colors.
8. Repeat step 6 using a different color of light each time, and observe how different parts of the earthworm react to each

color of light. Try this with different worms.

9. Remember, always record your results.

Can you answer the following questions from your observations?

1. Which parts of the earthworm seemed most sensitive to light?
2. What happened when you shined the light on the tail end, body, and head of the earthworm? Did the earthworm wriggle its tail end more when you shined a certain color of light on it? What color made the earthworm wriggle its tail end more than the other colors?
3. What happened when you shined the red light on the earthworm? How did the earthworm react to red compared to the other colors you shined on it?
4. Did all the earthworms react in the same way to the same color of light?
5. Do you think earthworms have nerve cells and senses?

Backyard Scientist solution:

You probably discovered that most of the earthworms reacted to the light by wriggling their tail ends vigorously. This response was probably most noticeable when the light struck the earthworm's head. You might try to keep track of how many times their tail ends were wriggling to the different colors in a 1-minute period, 2-minute period, 3-minute period, 4-minute period, and 5-minute period.

You should have observed that earthworms reacted more vigorously to the white light than they did to the other lights.

The sensory cells in a worm's skin are less sensitive to red light than to light of other colors. Red light is best for locating earthworms at night in the wild. You can see them quite well, and at the same time you will not alarm them. Worms will move away from blue lights.

Earthworms can get so used to bright light that they do not react. If you keep an earthworm in a well-lighted room for an hour or so, it will not respond even if a bright light is flashed on it.

As humans, we learn about the world around us from our senses. Our sense organs contain nerve cells. Some nerve cells are sensitive to light, others to sound, still others to heat, cold and pressure. Earthworms also have senses. Earthworms seem to sense light and sound even though they have no eyes or ears. Earthworms can sense the world around them. An earthworm has clusters of light-sensitive cells at its front end. This is the way an earthworm is guided to the surface of the ground. The worms respond to dim light by crawling toward it. They respond to bright light by crawling away from it. Now you know why earthworms come to the surface at night, but not during the day. Earthworms are also sensitive to a decrease in light.

You can also do this same experiment indoors. Place a worm on wet paper towels in a shallow container with edges. Keep it in a darkened room for a few minutes. Then repeat the above experiments with the flashlight.

Do Earthworms Prefer to Eat Certain Foods?

Gather the following supplies:

five or more deep plastic containers with wide mouths (Tupperware containers are good for this experiment.), plastic screen material or cloth, damp soil, fresh leaves from a variety of shrubs and trees, partially decaying leaves, vegetable leaves such as celery leaves, carrot tops, lettuce, cabbage, turnip greens, etc., baby food, fruit peelings, cornmeal or bread crumbs, coffee grounds, and lots of earthworms.

A tree guide would come in handy, but is optional. Make a chart to record which foods your earthworms liked best.

NOTE: This experiment will take 1 or 2 weeks.

Start experimenting.

1. Fill the containers with good, fresh, damp soil.
2. Number the containers 1, 2, 3, and so on.
3. Place two or three earthworms in each container.
4. Cover the containers with plastic screen.
5. Make a chart and record which leaves and foods you will be placing in container number 1, 2, 3, and so on. A tree guide will help you identify the different kinds of leaves you put in your containers. You can get a tree guide from the library.
6. Please wait until the next day to continue this experiment.

7. Now you are ready to begin the next part of the experiment.
8. Remove the plastic screen and put some food in the plastic containers. For example, take two fresh leaves of different kinds, moisten them, and put them on top of the soil in your earthworms' containers. Be sure to mark on your chart which leaves you put in each container. It might be fun to keep track of which leaves the worms liked best by observing the order in which they ate the leaves.
9. Use a few different foods for each container. When giving the earthworms food, be sure to moisten the food, and

put a thin covering of fresh soil over it after putting the food into the containers. Do not feed the earthworms too much food as the food may spoil. Two tablespoons of food every other week should be enough. Discard any food that the earthworms do not eat, or that has a bad smell, or is moldy.

10. Cover the containers again and let stand for one week or more.

11. Observe your earthworms at different times during the day and night, and note on your chart what is happening. At night, observe your worms through the sides of the container in a dim light.

12. From time to time be sure to check through the soil for young worms. Do not allow the container to become over-populated with worms. Put your extra worms in other containers or return them to their natural habitat.

Can you answer the following questions from your observations?

1. What did you observe the worms doing the day before you put any food or leaves into their containers?

2. Which leaves did your earthworms like best? Did the earthworms eat everything you fed them? Did they like certain food or leaves better than others?

3. Did some food or leaves remain uneaten?

4. Do you think the size of the leaves make a difference to the earthworms?

5. Do you think all earthworms have the same taste in leaves or food?

6. Were the earthworms more active during the day or at night?

Backyard Scientist solution:

During the first 24-hour period, the earthworms quickly got used to their new environment and began building their burrows. Did you discover that the earthworms definitely liked some leaves better than others? I have found the fresh leaves that earthworms like best are beech, maple, oak, lime, willow and horse chestnut. The decaying leaves that earthworms like are horse chestnut, willow, oak, lime and maple.

If you caught the worms at exactly the right time when you observed them at night through the sides of the container, you might have caught them partially out of their burrows and might actually have seen them nibbling at the pointed end of a leaf.

Did you notice that the food the earthworms did not like remained on the top of the soil?

I would like to know which leaves and foods your earthworms liked best. Please share the results of your experiments with me. Write to me at: Backyard Scientist, P.O. Box 16966, Irvine, CA 92713.

Why Do Earthworms Eat Soil and Organic Material?

Gather the following supplies:

several small zip-close plastic bags, labels for identifying the bags, pen or pencil, magnifying lens, white paper plate, small shovel, writing paper, earthworms, a table to work at, and some friends or family members.

NOTE: This experiment will take several days.

Start experimenting.

1. With friends or family, search for different types of soil in your yard. If you leave your yard, be sure to have an adult along. As you find different types of soil, use your shovel to place some in your zip-close specimen bags. Place one sample in each bag. Get different kinds of soils: damp, dry, sandy, loam or clay. These can be found in wooded areas, grassy areas, and around ponds or streams.

2. Be sure to make a label describing the soil and location from which you took it, and affix it to each sealed bag.

3. Now that you have gathered all your soil samples, it is time to analyze them. Empty the contents from one bag onto your white plate. Spread it out.
4. With your magnifying lens, search out all the different things you find in the sample and record your observations.
5. Return the sample to the bag it was in.
6. Repeat steps 3, 4, and 5 for each sample you gathered.
7. Find enough earthworms to place two in each sample bag that you filled.
8. Punch very small air holes in each bag.
9. Place the bags in a dark and cool place for a few days.
10. Remove the worms from the bags and release them into your garden, and then close the bags again.
11. Again, spread a soil sample on a plate and look through your magnifying lens to see what kind of things you find. Repeat this procedure with the other bags.
12. Compare these findings with the ones you recorded from your initial findings.

Can you answer the following questions from your observations?

1. What kind of particles did you first find in the soil samples?
2. Do you think worms would enjoy eating anything you found? Remember, worms like to eat foods that are different than the kinds of food you like to eat.
3. Were there observable differences in the contents of the soil before and after you added the earthworms?
4. What was missing after the earthworms were added and later released?
5. Does this mean the earthworms liked those things better than other things in the soil?

Backyard Scientist Solution:

Did you find soils that were mostly sand, or mostly clay? Did they contain bits of small rocks, plant roots, seeds and seed parts, insects (alive and dead), and leaves?

From your observations, you probably observed that earthworms like to eat bits of leaves, rotting seeds and dead insects for nourishment. This organic material, from something that was once alive, provides the earthworms with the nutrients they require. Soil containing organic material is ingested by the earthworms and passes through the worms' long digestive tract. Because the earthworm has such a small mouth, it prefers soft foods. Other foods have to be softened by moisture so the worm can suck them into its mouth.

From the earthworm's *pharynx* the food passes into the *esophagus.* There are several pairs of *calciterous* glands which secrete *calcium carbonate* into the esophagus. They function in the neutralization of acid soil as well as the elimination of excess carbonate from the blood.

Next, the food moves to the *crop*, which serves as a temporary storage place. From here it moves into the *gizzard*. Here, grains of ingested sand are ground by the thick and muscular walls. Food is then forced into the *intestine*. Glands secrete digestive chemicals and the digested food passes through the walls of the intestine and into the bloodstream. Wastes are expelled through the *anus*.

What Is in Sand and Soil That Makes It Habitable for Earthworms?

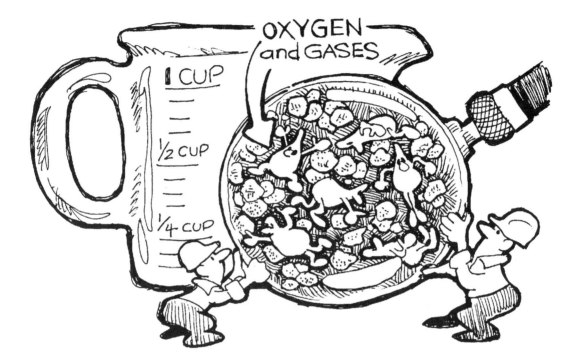

Gather the following supplies:

½ cup garden soil, cup of water, ½ cup sand (construction sand or river sand—do not use beach sand), pencil and paper, and two 1-cup see-through measuring cups.

Start experimenting.

1. Measure ½ cup of sand into one of the measuring cups.
2. Fill the other measuring cup with ½ cup of water.
3. Pour the water into the measuring cup containing the sand.

4. Look very carefully at the measuring cup of sand. Does it measure exactly 1 cup, or just a little less? Jot down your observation.
5. Pour out the sand and water. Thoroughly rinse out the measuring cup.

6. Measure ½ cup of garden soil into a measuring cup.
7. Fill the other measuring cup with ½ cup of water and pour it into the measuring cup of soil.
8. Look very carefully at the measuring cup containing the soil. Does it measure exactly 1 cup, or a little less? Record your observation.

Can you answer the following questions from your observations?

1. Did you discover that the sand measured less than a full cup even though you measured in ½ cup of sand and ½ cup of water (½ + ½ is supposed to equal 1)?
2. Did you have similar results with the garden soil?
3. Is a quantity of sand and soil completely solid when compared to a rock?

Backyard Scientist solution:

The ½ cup of sand or soil when combined with the ½ cup of water did not measure a full cup. There are spaces between the sand granules and the materials in the garden soil. These spaces are filled with air which, among other gases, contains oxygen. This is the source of oxygen the earthworms require to respire. Respiration is the process earthworms use to get oxygen into their systems and to rid their systems of waste gases. It might be fun to investigate how other living things accomplish this task.

A volume of soil and sand is usually about 25 percent air. The burrowing of earthworms in the soil significantly increases the amount of air in the soil. This helps to enrich the soil by providing oxygen so leaves and dead insects will decay faster.

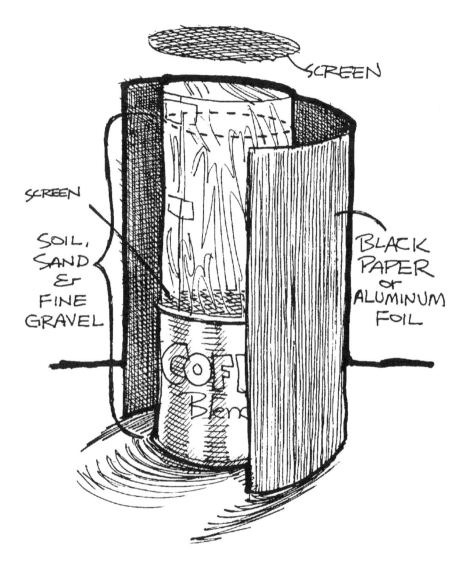

SCREEN

SCREEN

SOIL,
SAND
&
FINE
GRAVEL

BLACK
PAPER
or
ALUMINUM
FOIL

To find out more about how earthworms live, the best thing to do would be to watch them go about their business in their natural habitat. Because earthworms live underground in small burrows, this is not possible.

We will have to build a special habitat for them that will allow them to live as they do normally, yet allow us to observe their activities without disturbing them.

Gather the following supplies:

an empty coffee can (13-oz. to 16-oz. size), a 20 x 24-inch sheet of clear acetate (get this at your local art supply or stationery store), clear tape, a piece of plastic screen (like the kind on your windows), several rubber bands, some soil, sand and fine gravel, and an adult to help you. A clean, empty milk carton may be substituted for the coffee can.

CAUTION: IF USING THE COFFEE CAN, BE CAREFUL NOT TO CUT YOUR FINGERS.

Start building your observation habitat.

Have an adult help you build this.

1. Fill the empty coffee can or milk carton halfway with sand, soil, or fine gravel.
2. Cut the sheet of acetate to make a strip 20 inches by 12 inches. If the acetate is too thin, you should cut it 20 inches by 24 inches so you can double it. Have an adult help you cut this.
3. Roll the acetate into a tube to fit into the can. Hold the shape of the tube with a rubber band and tape the edges.
4. Cut a piece of screen to fit the diameter of the can.
5. Put the plastic screen on top of the soil in the can, then insert the tube into the can.
6. Fill the tube (habitat) with damp earth, not too wet, until it comes to within an inch of the top.

Now that the habitat is complete, you are ready to put it to use. Do the experiment on the following page.

Gather the following supplies:

the earthworm habitat you just constructed, two or three earthworms, some decaying leaves or other plant materials, a piece of plastic screen (window screen works well), a piece of black paper or aluminum foil large enough to completely wrap around the side of the tube, rubber bands, and pencil and paper for recording your observations.

NOTE: This experiment will take about a month.

Start experimenting.

1. Place your earthworms in their new habitat.
2. Cover the top with the screen and fasten it with rubber bands, so the earthworms can't get out.
3. Observe the earthworms' activities and record your observations.
4. After the earthworms have begun to burrow their tunnels, add a few rotted leaves or other plant material so they will have something to eat.
5. Cover the sides of the tube with the black paper or aluminum foil. Earthworms avoid light, so we want to make their habitat dark and as natural for them as possible.
6. Store your habitat in a cool, dark place. Keep the soil damp, but not wet.
7. Periodically remove the covering from your habitat and observe what the worms have done, and are doing. Replace the cover. Jot down your observations about their activities and behavior.
8. Check their food preferences by placing a few bits of lettuce, chopped onion, coffee grounds, or bits of fruit on the soil.

Can you answer the following questions from your observations?

1. When you removed the cover from the habitat, were the worms usually stretched out or curled up in a coil?
2. When you removed the cover to observe the earthworms, did they stay pretty much in place or try to burrow away from the light?
3. Where did you find the earthworms? Near the top of the habitat, at the bottom, or somewhere in the middle?
4. Which foods did the earthworms seem to prefer?

Backyard Scientist solution:

Are you getting lots of interesting information about what earthworms do and how they live? After only a few days, the earthworms began making a network of burrows to obtain food. Earthworms are slow, but very steady workers. You should release your earthworms after about thirty days.

Ideas for further experimenting.

Refill the habitat with layers of different kinds of soil, sand, and gravel. Add a new complement of earthworms and some food on top of the soil. Cover the sides and periodically remove the top of the habitat and observe. Cover the top and periodically remove the sides and observe. Do earthworms prefer to live in certain types of soil? What seems to happen to the soil they move as they burrow?

Do You Think Worms Need Oxygen and Moisture?

Gather the following supplies:

No supplies are necessary. Just ask some family members or friends to join you in putting on your thinking caps and using your observation skills. **SPECIAL NOTE: When looking for earthworms, watch out for snakes, centipedes, spiders and other dangerous animals.**

Start experimenting.

1. Go into your backyard or have an adult take you to a park.
2. Where, besides in the soil, might you expect to find earthworms? Try looking under dead logs or tree limbs, under rocks, and at the edges of sidewalks after a rain. Also try searching other places. *CAUTION: Watch out for* *spiders, snakes, centipedes and other dangerous animals.*
3. As a group, discuss why earthworms might be found in the places described in step 2. Also, based on what you have already learned about these interesting animals, where else might you expect to find them?

Can you answer the following questions from your observations?

1. Did you find earthworms in the places suggested in step 2?
2. Where else did you find them?
3. Why do you think you found earthworms in these places? Think about what earthworms need in order to live.

Backyard Scientist solution:

Earthworms are sometimes found under logs and rocks. After a heavy rain you will find them on and around sidewalks because their burrows have become flooded. All these places are dark, usually damp, and the right kind of foods are there for the earthworms. Oxygen that they need to respire is also abundant in these places. Earthworms do not breathe as we do. They respire (breathe) through their skin, exchanging carbon dioxide waste and taking in oxygen. Still another reason these are good places for earthworms is that they are protected there from their predators. Where else did you find earthworms? Why do you think you found them in those places?

Worms have no lungs or special breathing parts. Oxygen and carbon dioxide are respectively absorbed and exhausted through their skin. If water contains enough oxygen, worms can be immersed in it for limited periods of time and survive.

Are Earthworms Beneficial to Our Soil and for Growing Plants?

Gather the following supplies:

two plants (same size, age, and species), two pots (same size and kind), garden soil or peat moss, four to eight earthworms (small pots use two earthworms, large pots use four), ruler, paper, pencil, two labels, and a magnifying lens.

NOTE: This experiment will take from one to two months to complete.

Start experimenting.

1. Carefully plant one plant in each pot using your garden soil or peat moss.
2. Add the earthworms to one of the pots.
3. Label this pot "WITH EARTHWORMS."
4. Label the other pot "WITHOUT EARTHWORMS."
5. Place the pots side by side in a well-lighted area where the plants can thrive.
6. Water regularly. Always measure the water to be sure each plant receives exactly the same amount of water, and at the same time.
7. Observe the plants. Record your observations weekly for a month regarding height, fullness, and health of leaves and plants.
8. Use the magnifying lens to examine the soil in the two pots. Can you see the worms' castings? Record your observations.

Can you answer the following questions from your observations?

1. After a month went by, did you notice a difference in the two plants?
2. What differences did you observe?
3. What changes in the soil did you observe?
4. Do earthworms add anything to the soil?

Backyard Scientist solution:

Earthworms keep the soil loose as they burrow through it. The burrows allow air and water to enter deep into the soil. Earthworms also bring fresh soil up to the surface from down below. Earthworms are very good for soil. They have been called "nature's plowmen."

Because earthworms ingest such a large quantity of soil as they burrow, they leave *castings* which improve the chemical composition of the soil. Charles Darwin once estimated that an acre of farmland contains as many as 50,000 earthworms. In a year, they can overturn as much as 18 tons of soil per acre.

How Can Earthworms Help in Our Efforts to Recycle?

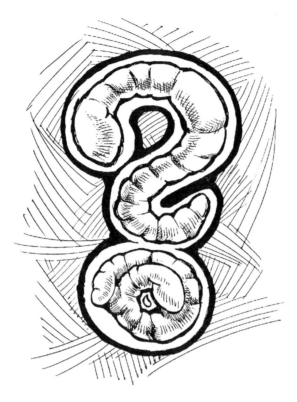

All you will need for this experiment is your brain. Let's all put on our thinking caps and review the material we learned in the experiments we did on earthworms. You may want to pull out any notes you made from your observations.

Can you answer the following questions from your observations?

1. Do earthworms make soil conditions more favorable for plant and crop growth?
2. How do earthworms take an active role in the recycling process?
3. How do earthworms help in decomposing materials?
4. What do you think would happen if these processes of decay and decomposition did not take place?
5. The earthworm definitely has, as we discovered, its own specific tasks relating to the environment. Do you think other animals have their own particular tasks as well? Can you list some examples?
6. Do you think all living things are involved in recycling?
7. Why do you think it is so fascinating to

study earthworms and their habits?

8. Can earthworms injure you?
9. Using your imagination, can you design another animal that is especially suited to living beneath the earth's surface, one that eats leaves and decomposed insects, etc., and has the same, or even more beneficial, characteristics than the earthworm?
10. Is good soil as important to earthworms as it is to people?

Backyard Scientist solution:

Earthworms, as they move through the soil, make tunnels that bring air into the soil. This process also mixes the different layers of soil, bringing lower layers up to or near the surface. Earthworms also add fertilizer to the soil as they eat small leaves, fruit peels and other organic matter.

Other animals also call the earth their home. However, they are not as broadly beneficial as are earthworms.

The soil is more than dirt to humans. It is the very foundation of our ability to sustain ourselves. In it, we grow the crops that feed us and the foods that feed the domesticated animals we use for food. Earthworms play a major role in making soils more favorable for good plant growth.

Earthworms are very efficient at *decomposition,* the breaking down of complex materials in their bodies. The earthworms excrete these materials, in much simpler form, back into the soil, making them available for simpler beneficial organisms.

If the process of decomposition did not take place, the basic chemicals needed to sustain life would remain locked up in the bodies of dead plants and animals forever. All animals play an important role in recycling. However, we humans are the most inefficient recyclers. We generate large amounts of trash and much of it that will not decompose, or may decompose into dangerous substances. Do you have a recycling program in your home? If you don't, why not take charge, plan and run one on your own? You may even be able to earn some spending money with the trash you recycle.

I think you would find it difficult to design an animal more suited to living in the environment the earthworm likes best and calls home. However, this was a good exercise to get you to use your imagination.

Earthworms are interesting to study because they are abundant, durable, easy to handle, and they can't harm you. They are also easy to contain, once caught.

Birds are also excellent recyclers. They eat many of the same types of organic material that earthworms eat. Many birds also like to eat earthworms. You will see birds hunting for earthworms after it has rained or the lawn has been watered, when the earthworms come to the surface because their burrows have become flooded. That is another subject, the *food chain*, that you can study. Birds also recycle by using bits of string, paper, and other materials to construct their nests. Birds and their habits, are still another interesting area of science to study.

A Thinking Experiment About Earthworms

Special note from the Backyard Scientist: Complete this exercise without looking at the answers at the end of this experiment. You may write your answers on a piece of paper, or if you are very young and can't write yet, tell your answers to an adult who will write them down for you. Don't worry if you don't know an answer. In science it is fine to make a guess. This is termed *hypothesizing*. Scientists do this all the time and then conduct research to prove or disprove the hypothesis.

1. In what soil conditions do earthworms like to live?
   - Damp soil?
   - Warm soil?
   - Cool soil?
   - Dry soil?
   - Sand?
   - Soil with lots of plant materials?
   - Damp, warm soil?
2. What do earthworms do when it gets very cold? Take a guess.
3. What time of day do earthworms become most active? During the day? At night?
4. Earthworms do not have eyes. What do you think would happen if you shined a flashlight on them during the night? Would the earthworms somehow feel the light rays? If so, what type of senses do earthworms use to feel light?
5. Do earthworms prefer to be dry or moist?

Backyard Scientist solution:

Earthworms prefer to live in damp, warm soil. When temperatures fall, earthworms burrow deeper into the soil where it is warmer. During periods of cold weather, they stay deep in their burrows and do not come to the surface.

Earthworms are most active during evening hours. While earthworms do not have eyes, they will sense the light from a flashlight on their bodies. Their skin covering contains special cells that are sensitive to light, and nerves carry this information to other special cells that act as a rudimentary brain. As soon as the earthworms feel the light from the flashlight, they will begin to go into their burrows. If they are too far away from it, they will start to make a new burrow.

Earthworms must keep their outer skin covering moist. That is the reason they will be more often found in damp soil.

I hope you enjoyed learning about earthworms and now have a better understanding of how they live and thrive. After doing the experiments in this book, you also became aware of how beneficial the earthworm is to mankind.

I am certain that you have many more unanswered questions about earthworms. You will have to do more research and science experiments to answer your excellent questions, the way real scientists do.

Here are some questions to help you get started on developing your own experiments.

1. Can you find the pulse of an earthworm?
2. What is the average pulse rate of an earthworm?
3. How do earthworms react to different temperatures?
4. Can earthworms move backwards?
5. How fast can earthworms move?
6. Are earthworms sensitive to touch?
7. Are earthworms referred to as cold-blooded animals?
8. What is the meaning of "cold-blooded animal"?
9. Do all parts of the earthworm's body react to touch in the same way?

Take these steps to set up your own experiment:

1. **Hypothesis**. Before you begin an experiment, you may have an idea, or a guess, about what you think will happen. Your results will help you decide if your hypothesis was right. The whole purpose of doing an experiment is to discover if you were right or wrong. Wrong answers in this case are not bad, because you learned something from them that you did not know before.
2. **Materials.** Before you begin experimenting, make a list of all the supplies you will need. This enables you to do some advance planning and makes you more efficient.
3. **Procedure.** Keep your experiment on track. Only test for one thing at a time. Be sure to keep all the variables (conditions) the same in your experiment. If you want to try a new variable, do a separate experiment.
4. **Observations.** This is a very important part of your experiment. Always keep track of your observations by recording them on a piece of paper or into a tape recorder. Recording information is a vital part of all experiments. This way you can compare your observations with those of someone else doing the same experiment. Repetition is very important in science. When you get the same answer repeatedly, it is a strong indicator that the research results are correct.
5. **Conclusion.** Take a good look at the results and see if they answer the question or support your hypothesis. Do you completely understand the results? You may discover that you need to do further experimenting to clear up any loose ends. The process of experimenting brings up new questions that have not been thought of before.
6. **Further research**. These are new questions that arise as a result of previous investigations that need to be answered.

For example, you may want to find out more about how an earthworm is put together. You may want to take one apart (dissect it). Dissection requires some special instruments and specially prepared earthworm specimens. It must also be done carefully, so you don't destroy any of the parts you wish to investigate. You never want to dissect a live earthworm. A labeled drawing of the anatomy of an earthworm is included elsewhere in this book.

Raising Earthworms for Profit

Raising earthworms for profit began back in the early fifties and has grown by some estimates to a multi-billion dollar industry. Thousands of people make all or part of their income raising these animals.

Raising earthworms is an excellent business for children to engage in. They will learn responsibility, and they will begin to learn the skills of running a small business.

Originally, earthworms were raised to satisfy the demand of sport fishermen who used them for bait. Today, in addition to this market, other markets have developed that include soil enrichment for organic gardens, ecologically safe conversion of organic waste to high-yield fertilizer, export to underdeveloped nations for farm soil enrichment, and food for pets, fish hatcheries, zoos, and tropical fish. You can probably think of other markets as well. Raising earthworms is a fascinating business that can be very profitable. It takes only a relatively few dollars to begin the business. The business can grow until it is quite large depending on the amount of effort you put into it.

No special skills or training are required to enter the commercial earthworm business. It can be run from the backyard, a garage, a lot or a farm. Be sure to check your local zoning laws for any restrictions before you begin.

There are a number of publications available on raising earthworms for profit. Check with your local library.

Get Your Official Backyard Scientist Certificate and Join the Backyard Scientist Club!

Just print your name and address on a slip of paper and state that you have completed all the experiments in the book. Include 52 cents in stamps and I will send you your official Backyard Scientist Certificate and enroll you in the Backyard Scientist Club. Also, The Backyard Scientist would like to know which experiments you liked best and why.

Write to: Backyard Scientist
                    P.O. Box 16966
                    Irvine, CA 92713

Get Ready for More Exciting Hands-on Science Experiments in Other Backyard Scientist Books

Each award winning and best selling book contains different and stimulating hands-on science experiments...that work. These exciting experiments require supplies that are commonly found in the home or that are readily available at very low cost.

The Original Backyard Scientist and **Backyard Scientist, Series One** give the 4- to 12-year-old investigator an excellent introduction to chemistry, physics and the solid sciences.

Backyard Scientist, Series Two will challenge and astonish the 9- to 14-year-old with exciting, fascinating and challenging experiments focusing on chemistry and physics.

Backyard Scientist, Series Three focuses the 4- to 12-year-old scientist on the life sciences.

Backyard Scientist, Series Four contains an exciting collection of hands-on science experiments that children of all ages will enjoy doing. It is an excellent resource for individual, family, group and classroom investigations. Many exciting aspects of chemistry and physics, are explored in these electrifying hands-on experiments.

Backyard Scientist It's Like Magic Super Crystal Kit allows children to use the scientific method to explore the unique properties of the nontoxic (when used as directed), environmentally safe chemical contained in the kit. Using simple arithmetic, children will make scientific comparisons. So much learning and a lot of fun at the same time!

Backyard Scientist books are available from school supply stores, museum shops, toy stores, bookstores, and many catalogs of educational materials.